The Gambino Crime

A Mafia Family Revealed

Filiquarian Publishing, LLC.

A Mafia Family Revealed

Filiquarian Publishing, LLC is publishing this edition of The Gambino Crime Family - A Mafia Family Revealed due to its status under the GNU Free Documentation License.

The cover of, The Gambino Crime Family - A Mafia Family Revealed and the "Biographiq" imprint is copyright 2008, Filiquarian Publishing, LLC.

Copyright (C) 2008 Filiquarian Publishing, LLC.
Permission is granted to copy, distribute and/or modify this document under the terms of the GNU Free Documentation License, Version 1.2 or any later version published by the Free Software Foundation; with no Invariant Sections, no Front-Cover Texts, and no Back-Cover Texts. A copy of the license is included in the section entitled "GNU Free Documentation License".

The photo on the cover is of a mugshot of Carlo Gambino taken by the New York City Police Department. It is being used here under the fair use clause of the United States copyright laws.

The Gambino Crime Family - A Mafia Family Revealed is available for free download at www.biographiq.com/bookd/GCF632

Filiquarian Publishing, LLC.

The Gambino Crime Family

A Mafia Family Revealed

The Gambino crime family is one of the "Five Families" that controls organized crime activities based in New York City, United States, within the nationwide criminal phenomenon known as the Mafia (or Cosa Nostra). Based in New York City, the group's operations extend to much of the eastern seaboard and all across the nation to California. Its illicit activities include labor racketeering, gambling, loansharking, extortion, murder for hire, solid and toxic waste dumping violations, construction, building and cement violations, fraud and wire fraud, hijacking, pier thefts and fencing.

A Mafia Family Revealed

History of the Gambino Crime Family

Origins

The origins of the Gambino crime family can be traced all the way back to the days of a criminal Neapolitan gang led by Pellegrino "Don Grino" Morano, which was taken over by Vincenzo Ingegni following the jailing of Morano in 1916. D'Aquila faced up against the forces of Giuseppe "Joe the Boss" Masseria and was killed around 1928, when the gang he had led passed into the hands of Alfred Mineo and Steve Ferrigno, at the height of the Prohibition era. The Castellammarese War, between rival New York bosses Masseria and Salvatore Maranzano, claimed many victims, including Mineo and Ferrigno who were ambushed and killed on November 5, 1930, outside of Ferrigno's home at 759 Pelham Parkway South. It was the latest in a long line of killings on both sides of the war, which would ultimately end with the deaths of both principals - Masseria in April 1931 and Maranzano five months later. The main beneficiary (and organizer of both hits) was

Charlie "Lucky" Luciano, who duly set about rearranging New York's organized crime and establishing the basis of the "Five Families", which became known as the Commission of the Cosa Nostra.

After the Castellammarese War

Following rief period under the control of Frank Scalise, the first recognized leader of what would become the Gambino family was Vincenzo "Vincent" Mangano, an old-school Mafia don in the style of Masseria and Maranzano, but one who was tolerated due to his close ties with Emil Camarda, the vice-president of the International Longshoremen's Association. Through the association, Mangano and the family controlled the New York and Brooklyn waterfront with activities ranging from extortion to union racketeering, as well as illegal gambling operations including horse betting, running numbers and lotteries. Mangano also established the City Democratic Club, ostensibly to promote bedrock American values but in reality as a cover for Murder, Inc., the notorious band of mainly Jewish hitmen who would do the bidding of the

Italian-American run families, for a price. Phil Mangano was a member, as was Albert Anastasia, known as the "Lord High Executioner". Around this time, Carlo Gambino was promoted within the organization, as was another future boss of the family, Gambino's brother-in-law Paul "Big Paul" Castellano.

Mangano Brothers Murdered

Anastasia and Mangano never entirely saw eye to eye. Mangano resented that Anastasia preferred to keep the company of various members of the other families, and on numerous occasions the two almost came to blows. This was only ever going to end badly for Mangano, and in April, 1951, Phil Mangano was discovered murdered, while his brother disappeared without a trace.

Called to answer for the crimes of which he was suspected by the other New York bosses, Anastasia never admitted to his involvement in the deaths of the Manganos but did claim that Vince had been planning to have him killed. Albert Anastasia had since begun running the family himself, and few in the organization found themselves inclined to depose one of the most feared killers of the age. Carlo Gambino, a wily character with designs on the leadership himself, maneuvered himself into position as underboss to Anastasia.

Anastasia Eliminated

The fortunes of the family around this time were closely linked to those of another - that run by Frank Costello, and which is known today as the Genovese crime family. Vito Genovese was a power-hungry underboss in the family and needed a way to remove the close ties between Costello and Anastasia, which provided solidarity in the National Crime Syndicate for the two bosses.

Genovese thus jumped on the 1952 killing of a Brooklyn man named Arnold Schuster, who Anastasia had had killed for the most minor of indiscretions (acting as a prosecution witness against a bank robber Anastasia didn't even know), as evidence that Anastasia was unbalanced and a threat to the syndicate. With Gambino secretly siding with Genovese against his own boss, the wheels were in motion for the removal of Anastasia.

First, Costello was attacked and wounded outside his apartment building on May 2, 1957. The attack shook Costello to the extent that he soon announced his retirement from the head of his family, turning affairs over to Genovese. Alleged shooter was Vincent "Chin" Gigante.

Six months later, on October 25, 1957, Anastasia was murdered while sitting in a barber's chair at the Park Sheraton Hotel on West 56th Street. Gambino ordered the hit himself. For many years, the murder was believed to have been committed by Joseph "Crazy Joe" Gallo. Later, Colombo crime family boss and Gallo foe, Carmine "Junior" Persico claimed credit. However, journalist Jerry Capeci in his online column "Gangland" claims that the murder was committed by a three-man hit team organized by Joseph "Joe the Blonde" Biondo. The team consisted of Stephen Grammauta, Stephen Armone and Arnold Wittenburg, a crew of Lower East Side heroin dealers.[1]

Anastasia's former underboss Carlo Gambino took the reins of the family, which from then on bore his name. Biondo was rewarded with the underboss position, which he kept until his death in 1966. Grammauta eventually became a caporegime in the 1990s.

Gambino Promotes the Family

Genovese was sent to prison for 15 years, where he would eventually die in 1969. The Gambino family soon became one of the most powerful families in the National Crime Syndicate, with close ties to Meyer Lansky's offshore gaming houses in Cuba and the Bahamas, a lucrative business for the Mafia. The failure of Joseph "Joe Bananas" Bonanno to kill off Gambino and the heads of other New York crime families in the aftermath of the Bonanno War, saw Gambino become the most powerful leader of the five families.

Gambino allegedly stretched his power as far as to organize the shooting of Joe Colombo, head of the Colombo crime family, on June 28, 1971. More likely, Colombo shooter Jerome Johnson was a lone nut attracted to Colombo for his Italian civil rights movement. Or as Michael Franzese, an informer later said, it may have been set up by rogue law enforcement. Colombo survived the shooting but remained in a coma until his death in 1977. He was buried next to Joseph Gallo. Johnson was killed by Colombo's bodyguard.

In either case, Gambino's influence stretched into behind-the-scenes control of the Lucchese crime family, led by Carmine "Mr. Gribbs" Tramunti. Gambino also allegedly influenced the selection of Frank "Funzi" Tieri as boss of the Genovese crime family, after the murder of Thomas Eboli, whom Gambino, allegedly, had had killed over a $4 million dollar drug debt.

On October 15, 1976, Gambino died of a heart attack, and control of the family passed not to the obvious choice, Underboss Aniello "Mr. Neil" Dellacroce, but to Gambino's brother in-law, Paul Castellano. Allies of Dellacroce were thoroughly unhappy about that move, but Dellacroce himself kept his men in line, and was kept on as Castellano's Underboss.

The FBI Closes In

The Dellacroce faction remained displeased, believing that Castellano had inherited the role rather than earning it. Castellano did retain a degree of muscle to keep Dellacroce's allies in check, including the notorious crew run by Anthony "Nino" Gaggi and Roy DeMeo, which were believed to commit something between 75-200 murders during Castellano's regime from the late 1970s and mid 1980s.

It was not a time for the family to be embroiled in inner turmoil and argument, as the Federal Bureau of Investigation had targeted the Gambino family as the easiest of the five families to infiltrate - FBI tapes obtained from a bug planted in a lamp on Castellano's kitchen table caught him discussing illegal deals with his subordinates, and by the early 1980s Castellano was up on a number of charges and faced with conviction. He let it be known that he wanted Carlo Gambino's son Thomas to take over the family should he be sent to jail, with Thomas Bilotti (Castellano's chauffeur and bodyguard) as his Underboss, which further enraged the Dellacroce faction.

In 1983, a federal indictment charged 13 members of the Gambino family with drug trafficking. This group included John Gotti's brother, Gene, and his best friend, Angelo "Quack Quack" Ruggiero, who got his nickname for his non-stop talking. The feds had in fact been listening in on his home phone conversations since 1980 - they had Ruggiero on tape discussing family business, making drug deals, and expressing contempt for Castellano. If Castellano knew they were dealing drugs, in violation of his no-drug policy, Ruggiero would be killed. By law, the accused were allowed transcripts of wiretap conversations to aid their defense, and Castellano demanded to be shown them, though Dellacroce did his best to put him off.

Dellacroce was by this time suffering from cancer, but with Ruggiero desperate for help, his friend John Gotti stood up for him. All the same, Castellano maintained that he wanted the transcripts, or he would have Ruggiero and Gotti removed. Gotti realized he had to act fast, and the death of his mentor Dellacroce on December 2, 1985, paved the way for him to take out Castellano.

John Gotti Takes Over

On December 16, Bilotti and Castellano were heading for a meeting with capo Frank DeCicco at the Sparks Steak House on East 46th Street, when they were gunned down by four unidentified men in the middle of rush hour. These men were later recognized and identified by Mob expert Jerry Capeci to be Angelo Ruggiero, John Carneglia, Vincent Artuso and Salvatore Scala.

Known as the "Dapper Don," Gotti was well-known for his hand-tailored suits and silk ties and his willingness to throw out sound bites to the media in a way unlike any Mafioss before him. He appointed DeCicco as his Underboss and promoted Ruggiero to Caporegime in charge of his old crew. At that time, Salvatore "Sammy the Bull" Gravano was allegedly elevated to Consigliere. Gotti favored holding meetings while walking in public places so that surveillance equipment could pick up visual images, but not the matters being discussed. His home in Howard Beach, Queens, was frequently seen on television. One of his neighbours during that time was John Favara, who disappeared after hitting Gotti's 12-year-old son with a car while he was riding his bike, and killing him instantly. Another neighbour was Gotti's dear friend and associate, Joseph "Big Joe" Massino, who was during the late 1980s recognized as the Underboss of the Bonanno crime family, and a strong candidate for leadership, for the imprisoned Boss Philip "Rusty" Rastelli.

Many mob leaders disapproved of his high-profile style, particularly Genovese crime family boss Vincent "Chin" Gigante, a former ally of Castellano, who allegedly conspired with Lucchese crime family leaders Vittorio "Vic" Amsuo and Anthony "Gaspipe" Casso, to put out a contract on Gotti's life. On April 13, 1986, a car bomb meant for Gotti, instead killed DeCicco.

Eventually, Gotti's brash demeanor and belief that he was untouchable (he was acquitted on federal charges three times, earning the nickname the "Teflon Don") proved his undoing. The FBI had managed to bug an apartment above the Ravenite Social Club in Little Italy, where an elderly widow let mobsters hold top-level meetings. Gotti was heard planning criminal activities and complaining about his underlings, including Salvatore "Sammy the Bull" Gravano, who upon hearing the tapes decided to turn state's evidence and testify against Gotti, and dozens of other mobsters, from all the Five Families.

On April 2, 1992, Gotti and current Consigliere Frank "Frankie Loc" LoCascio were convicted and received a sentence of life without parole.

The Family since Gotti

Gotti continued to rule the family from prison, while day-to-day operation of the family shifted to capos John "Jackie Nose" D'Amico and Nick Corozzo. The latter was due to take over as acting boss but was himself sentenced to eight years in prison on racketeering charges. Gotti's son, John "Junior" Gotti, took over as head of the family, but in 1998 he too was convicted of racketeering and sentenced to 77 months in jail.

A Mafia Family Revealed

When Gotti Sr died in prison in 2002, his brother Peter took over as boss, allegedly alongside D'Amico, but the family's fortunes have dwindled to a remarkable extent given their power a few short decades ago. Peter Gotti was imprisoned as well in 2003, as the leadership allegedly went to the current administration members, Nicholas "Little Nick" Corozzo, John "Jackie Nose" D'Amico and Joseph "Jo Jo" Corozzo.

As former rivals of John Gotti took completely over the Gambino Family, mostly due to the fact that the rest of Gotti's loyalists were either jailed or under indictments, and that Gotti, Sr died in prison in 2002, then-current head of white collar crimes and caporegime, Michael "Mikey Scars" DiLeonardo turned state's evidence due to encreased law enforcement and credible evidence toward his racketeering trial, and was forced to tesify against mobsters from all of the Five Families. One of the last Gotti supporters, DiLeonardo testifyed against among others Peter Gotti and Anthony "Sonny" Ciccone from 2003 to 2005, and disappeared into the Witness Protection Program. At the same time, Salvatore "Sammy the Bull" Gravano, Gotti's former Underboss, had evaded the program in 1995 and was arrested and jailed for operating an Ecstacy-ring that stretched from Arizona to New York City in 2003. During that same year, he was sentenced to 19 years in prison, ironically due to informants amongst his associates.

In 2005, Nicholas "Little Nick" Corozzo and his longtime underling Leonard "Lenny" DiMaria were released from prison after serving ten years for racketeering and loansharking charges in New York and Florida. That same year, US lawenforcement recognized Corozzo as the Boss of the Gambino crime family, with his brother Joseph "Jo Jo" Corozzo as the family Consigliere, Arnold "Zeke" Squitieri as the acting Underboss, and John "Jackie Nose" D'Amico as a highly regarded member with the Corozzo brothers.

From the year of 2005 and toward 2007, the federal authorities has accomplished the prosecution and conviction of prominent Gambino capos Arnold "Zeke" Squitieri, Gregory DePalma, George "Butters" DeCicco, Ronald "One Armed Ronnie" Trucchio, Domenico "Italian Dom" Cefalu, Salvatore "Tore" LoCascio and Joseph

"Sonny" Juliano, including dozens of their soldiers and their associates.

Today, the FBI and the US government estimates the family to consist of around 200 to 250 made men. While they are larger than most other mob families and exert a lot of influence they are not as powerful as they were in Carlo Gambino's day and have arguably been in a steady, gradual decline ever since his death.

Bosses of the Gambino Crime Family

* 1907–1917 — Pellegrino Morano (Brooklyn Camorra leader, jailed 1917, then deported)

* 1916–1928 — Salvatore "Toto" D'Aquila (what was left of the Brooklyn Camorra aligned with the D'Aquila group, killed by Joe Masseria October 10 or 28, 1928)

* 1928–1930 — Alfred "Al Mineo" Manfredi (killed during Castellammarese War November 5, 1930)

The Gambino Crime Family

* 1930–1931 — Francesco "Frank/Don Cheech" Scalise (demoted after Salvatore Maranzano was killed)

* 1931–1951 — Vincenzo "Vincent" Mangano (recognized as the first official boss of the family which would be the Gambino Family, disappeared April 15, 1951, allegedly killed by Albert Anastasia)

* 1951–1957 — Albert "Mad Hatter" Anastasia (former head of the infamous death-squad Murder Incorporated, stepped up after Mangano dissapeared, killed October 25, 1957, on orders of his Underboss Carlo Gambino)

* 1957–1976 — Carlo "Don Carlo" Gambino (family godfather, seized also the power of the Commission and recognized as the most powerful boss during his entire regime from the late 1950s and all the way up to the mid 1970s, died October 15, 1976, of natural causes)

* 1974–1976 — Paul "Big Paul" Castellano (acting boss) (Followed orders from his boss, Carlo Gambino, right upon his death in 1976)

A Mafia Family Revealed

* 1976–1985 — Paul "Big Paul" Castellano (originally a captain and Gambino's brother-in-law who was promoted by Gambino on his death bed, which triggered a small war between two of the family's factions, killed on the orders of rival John Gotti, December 16, 1985)

* 1986–2002 — John Gotti (most infamous boss recognized in the media, stepped up with younger regimes, caused great rivalry between him and two other families, jailed from 1990-2002, officially recognized boss, died June 10, 2002, while incarcerated)

* 1992–1996 — Ruling Committee/Panel (aides to acting boss) Nicholas "Little Nick" Corozzo 1992-96 (jailed), Leonard "Lenny" DiMaria 1992-96 (jailed), John "Jackie Nose "DAmico 1992-96

* 1996–2002 — Ruling Committee/Panel John "Jackie Nose" D'Amico 1996-98 (jailed), Peter "One Eye" Gotti 1996-1999 (promoted), Louis "Big Lou" Vallario 1996-2002, Stephen "Stevie Coogan" Grammauta 1996-2002, Michael "Mikey Scars" DiLeonardo 1996-2002 (jailed 2002,

The Gambino Crime Family

defected November 2002) (Committee/Panel disbanded 2002, with death of longtime Don and Godfather, John Gotti)

* 1992–1999 — John A. Gotti Jr. aka John "Junior" Gotti (acting boss) (jailed 1999)

* 1999–2002 — Peter "One Eye" Gotti (acting boss)

* 2002–2003 — Peter "One Eye" Gotti (recognized as official boss, jailed 2002)

* 2002–2005 — Arnold "Zeke" Squitieri (acting boss)

* 2005–present — John "Jackie Nose" D'Amico (acting boss), Domenico "Italian Dom" Cefalu (acting underboss), Joseph "Jo Jo" Corozzo (consigliere)

* 2005–2006 — Nicholas "Little Nick" Corozzo (possibly the official sitting boss)

* 2006–2007 — Nicholas "Little Nick" Corozzo (Boss), Jackie "Nose" D'Amico (street

boss/caporegime), Domenico "Italian Dom" Cefalu (underboss, arrested on violation of his parole, in custody), Arnold "Zeke" Squitieri (acting underboss), Joseph "Jo Jo" Corozzo (consigliere)

* 2007–2008 — Nicholas "Little Nick" Corozzo (Boss), Jackie "Nose" D'Amico (street boss/caporegime), Leonard "Lenny" DiMaria (street boss/caporegime)On strict supervised release until 2008., Arnold "Zekey" Squitieri (acting underboss), Joseph "Jo Jo" Corozzo (consigliere)

* 2008–present — Nicholas "Little Nick" Corozzo (Boss), John "Jackie Nose" D'Amico (street boss), Arnold "Zekey" Squitieri (underboss), Joseph "Jo Jo" Corozzo (consigliere) (present regime-hierarchy 2008)

Current Family Leaders

* Nicholas "Little Nick" Corozzo - Capo, former rival of John Gotti and Boss of the Gambino crime family. Brother of Consigliere Joseph Corozzo, uncle of Joseph Jr. and the current head of the

caporegimes. Currently resides in Bellmore, Long Island.

* John "Jackie Nose" D'Amico - Capo, took over the old John Gotti crew in the early 1990s, operated in Queens and Brooklyn with labor racketeering, loansharking, extortion and murder. Currently an alleged street boss or acting boss along with the Corozzo brothers.

* Arnold "Squiggy" Squitieri - Underboss, longtime caporegime in the Gambino crime family, used to operate in Manhattan, Queens and Brooklyn with drug trafficking during the 1980s. Now he's currently promoted to Underboss.

* Joseph "Jo Jo" Corozzo - Current Consigliere and brother of Nicholas Corozzo, with alleged loansharking and illegal gambling operations in Manhattan and Queens. Held his position since 1992 as a former rival of John Gotti.

Current Family Capos

* Nicholas "Little Nick" Corozzo - Capo and Boss of the Gambino crime family. Brother of

A Mafia Family Revealed

Consigliere Joseph Corozzo, uncle of Joseph Jr. and the current head of the caporegimes. Currently resides in Bellmore, Long Island.

* John "Jackie Nose" D'Amico - Capo, took over the old John Gotti crew in the early 1990s, operated in Queens and Brooklyn with labor racketeering, loansharking, extortion and murder. Currently an alleged street boss or acting boss along with the Corozzo brothers.

* Thomas "Tommy" Gambino - Capo, son of former family godfather Carlo Gambino. Crew originally based in Brooklyn, Queens and Manhattan. Controls the racketeering in the Garment District.

* Leonard "Lenny" DiMaria - Capo, personal right-hand-man for Nicholas Corozzo since early 1970s. Operates in Brooklyn and Manhattan with racketeering and loansharking. Alleged racketeering operations in Florida.

* Thomas "Tommy Sneakers" Cacciopoli - Capo in the New Jersey faction of the Gambinos.

The Gambino Crime Family

* Domenico "Italian Dom" Cefalu - Former Underboss. The Sicilian faction-leader of the family, Cefalu is born in Italy. Currently imprisoned on violation of his parole.

* Daniel "Danny" Marino - Capo of the Gambinos' Queens faction with labor and construction racketeering operations. A longtime rival of John Gotti, Marino was involved in the murder-conspiracy that killed Frank DeCicco instead of Gotti in 1986.

* Anthony "Sonny" Ciccone - Capo. A legend on the Brooklyn waterfront and dock boss, now serving a long prison sentence.

* Salvatore "Vinny Papa" Ricchiettore - Acting Capo and current dock boss on behalf of Anthony Ciccone on the Brooklyn waterfront. Longtime member of the Gambino crime family.

* George "Butters" DeCicco - Capo and brother of former Gambino Underboss, Frank DeCicco. A loyalist to John Gotti, DeCicco has been operating out of the Staten Island and Brooklyn factions of

the family with loansharking since the 1980s. Currently on trial.

* Eugene "Gene" Gotti - Capo, imprisoned for drug-trafficking, loansharking, murder and extortion. Brother of John, Peter, Vincent Gotti and Richard. Gene Gotti is serving 50 to 60 years in prison, but is in charge of all Gambino family loansharking-business in New York City.

* Richard "Richie" Gotti - Capo of the Manhattan side. Brother of John Gotti, Peter, Gene and Vincent. Controls loansharking, extortion and garbage routs. Waste management consultant in Manhattan.

* Salvatore "Fat Sally" Scala - Capo with extortion, racketeering and loansharking operations based in the Queens, New York faction. Former heroin-trafficker and recognized by law enforcement as one of the designated shooters in the 1985 murders of Paul Castellano and Thomas Bilotti.

* Louis "Louie Bracciole" Ricco - Caporegime, controls illegal gambling, loansharking and

racketeering in one half of the Bronx, as well as operating out of the New Jersey and Brooklyn factions of the family.

* Salvatore "Tore" LoCascio - Capo - Son of the imprisoned Consigliere, Frank "Frankie Loc" LoCascio. Control of the other half of the Bronx faction. Used to operate within pornography that earned so much as $350 million a year, until he was prosecuted in 2003.

* George "Fat Georgie" Remini - Capo with illegal activities in the Manhattan and Queens wing. Apparently a top protege of Thomas "Tommy" Gambino. Died in March, 2007 of natural causes.

* Ronald "One Armed Ronnie" Trucchio - Capo with control of The Ozone Park Boys, used to operate in Queens, New York with a $30 million-a-year illegal gambling operation. Sentenced to life imprisonment in 2005.

* Stephen "Stevie Coogan" Grammauta - Caporegime in the Manhattan faction of the Gambino crime family. Recognized by Jerry

Capeci as one of the real shooters in the murder of Albert Anastasia in 1957, served as acting boss in the family's Ruling Committee/Panel from 1996 to 2002.

* Louis "Big Lou" Vallario - Capo, served from 1996 to 2002 as acting boss in the Family's Ruling Committee/Panel. Took over the crew of Sam Gravano in the 1980s. One of the last aides to John Gotti. Controls crew in Bensonhurst, Brooklyn.

* Joseph "Sonny" Juliano - Capo in the Brooklyn faction of the Gambino crime family with illegal gambling, loansharking, fraud and wire fraud activities. Used to manage and operate a multi-million-dollar illegal gambling ring in 30 different locations in New York City.

* Vincent "Vinny the Shrimp" Corrao - Capo with illegal gambling and narcotics operations. Crew originally based in Brooklyn.

* Vincent "Little Vinny" Artuso - Capo with control of the Palm Beach, Florida faction of the Gambino family. Former drug trafficker and

recognized by Jerry Capeci as one of the four designated shooters in the murder of Paul Castellano in 1985.

* Anthony "Tony Pep" Trentacosta - Caporegime in the South Florida faction of the family. Former friend of John Gotti, used to run a gasoline racket that cost the US government $1 billion in tax dollars during the 1980s.

Government Informants

* Salvatore "Sammy the Bull" Gravano, Underboss

* Michael "Mikey Scars" DiLeonardo, Caporegime

* Dominic "Fat Dom" Borghese, Soldier

* Primo Cassarino, Soldier

* Joseph D'Angelo, Soldier

* Frank "Frankie Fap" Fappiano, Soldier

A Mafia Family Revealed

* Willie Boy Johnson, Associate

* Dominick "Big Dom" LoFaro, Associate

* Frank "Red" Scollo, Associate

* Lewis N. Wilson, Providence drug kingpen

Gambino Family Mobsters

* Albert "Lord High Executioner" Anastasia

* Anthony "Tough Tony" Anastasio

* Thomas Bilotti

* Robert "Bobby Cabert" Bisaccia

* Bartholomew "Bobby" Boriello

* Paul Castellano - former Boss

* Roberto Cirelli- former capo

* John Cody

The Gambino Crime Family

* James Coonan

* Thomas DeBrizzi

* Frank DeCicco

* Aniello "Neil" Dellacroce

* Brian "Burns" Donahue

* Roy Demeo

* William "Billy Batts" Devino

* Michael "Mikey Scars" DiLeonardo

* James "Jimmy Brown" Failla

* Carmine "Charley Wagons" Fatico

* Mickey Featherstone

* Thomas "Tommy" Gambino - longtime Caporegime

* John "Dapper Don" Gotti

A Mafia Family Revealed

* John "Junior" Gotti, Jr.

* Salvatore "Sammy the Bull" Gravano - Former Underboss turned government witness

* Joseph Ianuzzi

* International Longshoremen's Association

* Edward Lino - former Capo

* Ray Scipione - Atlantic City operations

* Carmine "Doctor" Lombardozzi

* Michael Mandaglio

* Ralph "Ralphie Bones" Mosca - former caporegime

* [[Thomas [Spade] Muschio [Soldier]

* Frank Piccolo - former caporegime

* Anthony "Fat Andy" Ruggiano

* Angelo "Quack Quack" Ruggiero

* Anthony Scotto

* Michele "The Shark" Sindona

* Louis "Big Lou" Vallario

* Uriah "Scarface" Koleski

* Michael "Remo" Cruz

* Justin "Maddogg" Reese

Gambino Family Mafia Trials

* Mafia Commission Trial

* Pizza Connection Trial

Gambino Family Social Clubs

* Bergin Hunt and Fish Club

* Gemini Lounge

* Ravenite Social Club

In Popular Culture

* Mr. Moran is a song about Salvatore "Sammy the Bull" Gravano on the album A Jackknife to a Swan by the ska-core group The Mighty Mighty Bosstones.

* In the American Midwest, there is a franchise pizza restaurant called Gambino's Pizza.

* Rapper Raekwon recasts the Wu-Tang Clan as an Italian mafioso family dubbed the "Wu-Gambinos" on his debut album Only Built 4 Cuban Linx...

* In his song "Last Real Nigga Alive," Nas raps about his infamous feud with Jay-Z. In one line he says "...'Cause in order for him to be the don/ Nas had to go/ the Gam-b-i-n-o rules, I understood..."

Further Reading

* Capeci, Jerry. The Complete Idiot's Guide to the Mafia. Indianapolis: Alpha Books, 2002. ISBN 0-02-864225-2

* Davis, John H. Mafia Dynasty: The Rise and Fall of the Gambino Crime Family. New York: HarperCollins, 1993. ISBN 0-06-016357-7

* Jacobs, James B., Christopher Panarella and Jay Worthington. Busting the Mob: The United States Vs. Cosa Nostra. New York: NYU Press, 1994. ISBN 0-8147-4230-0

* Maas, Peter. Underboss: Sammy the Bull Gravano's Story of Life in the Mafia. New York: HarperCollins Publishers, 1997. ISBN 0-06-093096-9

* Raab, Selwyn. Five Families: The Rise, Decline, and Resurgence of America's Most Powerful Mafia Empires. New York: St. Martin Press, 2005. ISBN 0-312-30094-8

A Mafia Family Revealed

The Gambino Crime Family

GNU Free Documentation License

Version 1.2, November 2002

Copyright (C) 2000,2001,2002 Free Software Foundation, Inc.
51 Franklin St, Fifth Floor, Boston, MA 02110-1301 USA
Everyone is permitted to copy and distribute verbatim copies of this license document, but changing it is not allowed.

0. PREAMBLE

The purpose of this License is to make a manual, textbook, or other functional and useful document "free" in the sense of freedom: to assure everyone the effective freedom to copy and redistribute it, with or without modifying it, either commercially or noncommercially. Secondarily, this License preserves for the author and publisher a way to get credit for their work, while not being considered responsible for modifications made by others.

This License is a kind of "copyleft", which means that derivative works of the document must themselves be free in the same sense. It complements the GNU General Public License, which is a copyleft license designed for free software.

We have designed this License in order to use it for manuals for free software, because free software needs free documentation: a free program should come with manuals providing the same freedoms that the software does. But this License is not limited to software manuals; it can be used for any textual work, regardless of subject matter or whether it is published as a printed book. We recommend this License principally for works whose purpose is instruction or reference.

A Mafia Family Revealed

1. APPLICABILITY AND DEFINITIONS

This License applies to any manual or other work, in any medium, that contains a notice placed by the copyright holder saying it can be distributed under the terms of this License. Such a notice grants a world-wide, royalty-free license, unlimited in duration, to use that work under the conditions stated herein. The "Document", below, refers to any such manual or work. Any member of the public is a licensee, and is addressed as "you". You accept the license if you copy, modify or distribute the work in a way requiring permission under copyright law.

A "Modified Version" of the Document means any work containing the Document or a portion of it, either copied verbatim, or with modifications and/or translated into another language.

A "Secondary Section" is a named appendix or a front-matter section of the Document that deals exclusively with the relationship of the publishers or authors of the Document to the Document's overall subject (or to related matters) and contains nothing that could fall directly within that overall subject. (Thus, if the Document is in part a textbook of mathematics, a Secondary Section may not explain any mathematics.) The relationship could be a matter of historical connection with the subject or with related matters, or of legal, commercial, philosophical, ethical or political position regarding them.

The "Invariant Sections" are certain Secondary Sections whose titles are designated, as being those of Invariant Sections, in the notice that says that the Document is released under this License. If a section does not fit the above definition of Secondary then it is not allowed to be designated as Invariant. The Document may contain zero Invariant Sections. If the Document does not identify any Invariant Sections then there are none.

The "Cover Texts" are certain short passages of text that are listed, as Front-Cover Texts or Back-Cover Texts, in the notice that says that the Document is released under this License. A Front-Cover Text may be at most 5 words, and a Back-Cover Text may be at most 25 words.

The Gambino Crime Family

A "Transparent" copy of the Document means a machine-readable copy, represented in a format whose specification is available to the general public, that is suitable for revising the document straightforwardly with generic text editors or (for images composed of pixels) generic paint programs or (for drawings) some widely available drawing editor, and that is suitable for input to text formatters or for automatic translation to a variety of formats suitable for input to text formatters. A copy made in an otherwise Transparent file format whose markup, or absence of markup, has been arranged to thwart or discourage subsequent modification by readers is not Transparent. An image format is not Transparent if used for any substantial amount of text. A copy that is not "Transparent" is called "Opaque".

Examples of suitable formats for Transparent copies include plain ASCII without markup, Texinfo input format, LaTeX input format, SGML or XML using a publicly available DTD, and standard-conforming simple HTML, PostScript or PDF designed for human modification. Examples of transparent image formats include PNG, XCF and JPG. Opaque formats include proprietary formats that can be read and edited only by proprietary word processors, SGML or XML for which the DTD and/or processing tools are not generally available, and the machine-generated HTML, PostScript or PDF produced by some word processors for output purposes only.

The "Title Page" means, for a printed book, the title page itself, plus such following pages as are needed to hold, legibly, the material this License requires to appear in the title page. For works in formats which do not have any title page as such, "Title Page" means the text near the most prominent appearance of the work's title, preceding the beginning of the body of the text.

A section "Entitled XYZ" means a named subunit of the Document whose title either is precisely XYZ or contains XYZ in parentheses following text that translates XYZ in another language. (Here XYZ stands for a specific section name mentioned below, such as "Acknowledgements", "Dedications", "Endorsements", or "History".) To "Preserve the Title" of such a section when you modify the Document means that it remains a section "Entitled XYZ" according to this definition.

A Mafia Family Revealed

The Document may include Warranty Disclaimers next to the notice which states that this License applies to the Document. These Warranty Disclaimers are considered to be included by reference in this License, but only as regards disclaiming warranties: any other implication that these Warranty Disclaimers may have is void and has no effect on the meaning of this License.

2. VERBATIM COPYING

You may copy and distribute the Document in any medium, either commercially or noncommercially, provided that this License, the copyright notices, and the license notice saying this License applies to the Document are reproduced in all copies, and that you add no other conditions whatsoever to those of this License. You may not use technical measures to obstruct or control the reading or further copying of the copies you make or distribute. However, you may accept compensation in exchange for copies. If you distribute a large enough number of copies you must also follow the conditions in section 3.

You may also lend copies, under the same conditions stated above, and you may publicly display copies.

3. COPYING IN QUANTITY

If you publish printed copies (or copies in media that commonly have printed covers) of the Document, numbering more than 100, and the Document's license notice requires Cover Texts, you must enclose the copies in covers that carry, clearly and legibly, all these Cover Texts: Front-Cover Texts on the front cover, and Back-Cover Texts on the back cover. Both covers must also clearly and legibly identify you as the publisher of these copies. The front cover must present the full title with all words of the title equally prominent and visible. You may add other material on the covers in addition. Copying with changes limited to the covers, as long as they preserve the title of the Document and satisfy these conditions, can be treated as verbatim copying in other respects.

If the required texts for either cover are too voluminous to fit legibly, you should put the first ones listed (as many as fit reasonably) on the actual cover, and continue the rest onto adjacent pages.

The Gambino Crime Family

If you publish or distribute Opaque copies of the Document numbering more than 100, you must either include a machine-readable Transparent copy along with each Opaque copy, or state in or with each Opaque copy a computer-network location from which the general network-using public has access to download using public-standard network protocols a complete Transparent copy of the Document, free of added material. If you use the latter option, you must take reasonably prudent steps, when you begin distribution of Opaque copies in quantity, to ensure that this Transparent copy will remain thus accessible at the stated location until at least one year after the last time you distribute an Opaque copy (directly or through your agents or retailers) of that edition to the public.

It is requested, but not required, that you contact the authors of the Document well before redistributing any large number of copies, to give them a chance to provide you with an updated version of the Document.

4. MODIFICATIONS

You may copy and distribute a Modified Version of the Document under the conditions of sections 2 and 3 above, provided that you release the Modified Version under precisely this License, with the Modified Version filling the role of the Document, thus licensing distribution and modification of the Modified Version to whoever possesses a copy of it. In addition, you must do these things in the Modified Version:

* A. Use in the Title Page (and on the covers, if any) a title distinct from that of the Document, and from those of previous versions (which should, if there were any, be listed in the History section of the Document). You may use the same title as a previous version if the original publisher of that version gives permission.
* B. List on the Title Page, as authors, one or more persons or entities responsible for authorship of the modifications in the Modified Version, together with at least five of the principal authors of the Document (all of its principal authors, if it has fewer than five), unless they release you from this requirement.
* C. State on the Title page the name of the publisher of the Modified Version, as the publisher.
* D. Preserve all the copyright notices of the Document.

A Mafia Family Revealed

   * E. Add an appropriate copyright notice for your modifications adjacent to the other copyright notices.
   * F. Include, immediately after the copyright notices, a license notice giving the public permission to use the Modified Version under the terms of this License, in the form shown in the Addendum below.
   * G. Preserve in that license notice the full lists of Invariant Sections and required Cover Texts given in the Document's license notice.
   * H. Include an unaltered copy of this License.
   * I. Preserve the section Entitled "History", Preserve its Title, and add to it an item stating at least the title, year, new authors, and publisher of the Modified Version as given on the Title Page. If there is no section Entitled "History" in the Document, create one stating the title, year, authors, and publisher of the Document as given on its Title Page, then add an item describing the Modified Version as stated in the previous sentence.
   * J. Preserve the network location, if any, given in the Document for public access to a Transparent copy of the Document, and likewise the network locations given in the Document for previous versions it was based on. These may be placed in the "History" section. You may omit a network location for a work that was published at least four years before the Document itself, or if the original publisher of the version it refers to gives permission.
   * K. For any section Entitled "Acknowledgements" or "Dedications", Preserve the Title of the section, and preserve in the section all the substance and tone of each of the contributor acknowledgements and/or dedications given therein.
   * L. Preserve all the Invariant Sections of the Document, unaltered in their text and in their titles. Section numbers or the equivalent are not considered part of the section titles.
   * M. Delete any section Entitled "Endorsements". Such a section may not be included in the Modified Version.
   * N. Do not retitle any existing section to be Entitled "Endorsements" or to conflict in title with any Invariant Section.
   * O. Preserve any Warranty Disclaimers.

If the Modified Version includes new front-matter sections or appendices that qualify as Secondary Sections and contain no material copied from the Document, you may at your option designate some or all of these sections as invariant. To do this, add their titles to the list of Invariant Sections in the

The Gambino Crime Family

Modified Version's license notice. These titles must be distinct from any other section titles.

You may add a section Entitled "Endorsements", provided it contains nothing but endorsements of your Modified Version by various parties--for example, statements of peer review or that the text has been approved by an organization as the authoritative definition of a standard.

You may add a passage of up to five words as a Front-Cover Text, and a passage of up to 25 words as a Back-Cover Text, to the end of the list of Cover Texts in the Modified Version. Only one passage of Front-Cover Text and one of Back-Cover Text may be added by (or through arrangements made by) any one entity. If the Document already includes a cover text for the same cover, previously added by you or by arrangement made by the same entity you are acting on behalf of, you may not add another; but you may replace the old one, on explicit permission from the previous publisher that added the old one.

The author(s) and publisher(s) of the Document do not by this License give permission to use their names for publicity for or to assert or imply endorsement of any Modified Version.

5. COMBINING DOCUMENTS

You may combine the Document with other documents released under this License, under the terms defined in section 4 above for modified versions, provided that you include in the combination all of the Invariant Sections of all of the original documents, unmodified, and list them all as Invariant Sections of your combined work in its license notice, and that you preserve all their Warranty Disclaimers.

The combined work need only contain one copy of this License, and multiple identical Invariant Sections may be replaced with a single copy. If there are multiple Invariant Sections with the same name but different contents, make the title of each such section unique by adding at the end of it, in parentheses, the name of the original author or publisher of that section if known, or else a unique number. Make the same adjustment to the section titles in the list of Invariant Sections in the license notice of the combined work.

A Mafia Family Revealed

In the combination, you must combine any sections Entitled "History" in the various original documents, forming one section Entitled "History"; likewise combine any sections Entitled "Acknowledgements", and any sections Entitled "Dedications". You must delete all sections Entitled "Endorsements."

6. COLLECTIONS OF DOCUMENTS

You may make a collection consisting of the Document and other documents released under this License, and replace the individual copies of this License in the various documents with a single copy that is included in the collection, provided that you follow the rules of this License for verbatim copying of each of the documents in all other respects.

You may extract a single document from such a collection, and distribute it individually under this License, provided you insert a copy of this License into the extracted document, and follow this License in all other respects regarding verbatim copying of that document.

7. AGGREGATION WITH INDEPENDENT WORKS

A compilation of the Document or its derivatives with other separate and independent documents or works, in or on a volume of a storage or distribution medium, is called an "aggregate" if the copyright resulting from the compilation is not used to limit the legal rights of the compilation's users beyond what the individual works permit. When the Document is included in an aggregate, this License does not apply to the other works in the aggregate which are not themselves derivative works of the Document.

If the Cover Text requirement of section 3 is applicable to these copies of the Document, then if the Document is less than one half of the entire aggregate, the Document's Cover Texts may be placed on covers that bracket the Document within the aggregate, or the electronic equivalent of covers if the Document is in electronic form. Otherwise they must appear on printed covers that bracket the whole aggregate.

The Gambino Crime Family

8. TRANSLATION

Translation is considered a kind of modification, so you may distribute translations of the Document under the terms of section 4. Replacing Invariant Sections with translations requires special permission from their copyright holders, but you may include translations of some or all Invariant Sections in addition to the original versions of these Invariant Sections. You may include a translation of this License, and all the license notices in the Document, and any Warranty Disclaimers, provided that you also include the original English version of this License and the original versions of those notices and disclaimers. In case of a disagreement between the translation and the original version of this License or a notice or disclaimer, the original version will prevail.

If a section in the Document is Entitled "Acknowledgements", "Dedications", or "History", the requirement (section 4) to Preserve its Title (section 1) will typically require changing the actual title.

9. TERMINATION

You may not copy, modify, sublicense, or distribute the Document except as expressly provided for under this License. Any other attempt to copy, modify, sublicense or distribute the Document is void, and will automatically terminate your rights under this License. However, parties who have received copies, or rights, from you under this License will not have their licenses terminated so long as such parties remain in full compliance.

10. FUTURE REVISIONS OF THIS LICENSE

The Free Software Foundation may publish new, revised versions of the GNU Free Documentation License from time to time. Such new versions will be similar in spirit to the present version, but may differ in detail to address new problems or concerns. See http://www.gnu.org/copyleft/.

Each version of the License is given a distinguishing version number. If the Document specifies that a particular numbered version of this License "or any later version" applies to it, you have the option of following the terms

A Mafia Family Revealed

and conditions either of that specified version or of any later version that has been published (not as a draft) by the Free Software Foundation. If the Document does not specify a version number of this License, you may choose any version ever published (not as a draft) by the Free Software Foundation.

How to use this License for your documents

To use this License in a document you have written, include a copy of the License in the document and put the following copyright and license notices just after the title page:

Copyright (c) YEAR YOUR NAME.
Permission is granted to copy, distribute and/or modify this document under the terms of the GNU Free Documentation License, Version 1.2 or any later version published by the Free Software Foundation; with no Invariant Sections, no Front-Cover Texts, and no Back-Cover Texts. A copy of the license is included in the section entitled "GNU
Free Documentation License".

If you have Invariant Sections, Front-Cover Texts and Back-Cover Texts, replace the "with...Texts." line with this:

with the Invariant Sections being LIST THEIR TITLES, with the Front-Cover Texts being LIST, and with the Back-Cover Texts being LIST.

If you have Invariant Sections without Cover Texts, or some other combination of the three, merge those two alternatives to suit the situation.

If your document contains nontrivial examples of program code, we recommend releasing these examples in parallel under your choice of free software license, such as the GNU General Public License, to permit their use in free software.

Lightning Source UK Ltd.
Milton Keynes UK
UKOW031838060513

210270UK00009B/95/P